ALL NEW CRAFTS FOR

VALENTINE'S DAY

By Kathy Ross

illustrated by Barbara Leonard

The Millbrook Press
Brookfield, Connecticut

For my sweetheart, Tom
KR

For David
BL

Library of Congress Cataloging-in-Publication Data
Ross, Kathy (Katharine Reynolds), 1948-
All new crafts for Valentine's day / Kathy Ross ; illustrated by
Barbara Leonard.
p. cm. — (All new holiday crafts for kids)
Summary: Provides instructions for creating a variety of Valentine's Day
crafts, including cards, bookmarks, bracelets, Valentine holders,
magnets, and more.
ISBN 0-7613-2553-0 (lib. bdg.) — ISBN 0-7613-1576-4 (pbk.)
1. Valentine decorations—Juvenile literature. 2.
Handicraft—Juvenile literature. [1. Valentine decorations. 2.
Handicraft.] I. Leonard, Barbara, ill. II. Title. III. Series.
TT900.V34 R678 2002   745.594'1618—dc21   2002001930

Published by
The Millbrook Press, Inc.
2 Old New Milford Road
Brookfield, Connecticut 06804
www.millbrookpress.com

Printed in the United States of America
lib: 5 4 3 2 1
pbk: 5 4 3 2 1

Contents

These wearable valentines are so easy to do you might want to make one for each person in your class!

Button Nose Valentine

Here is what you need:

red and pink felt

red, purple, or pink yarn

thin ribbon and trims

cereal box cardboard

wiggle eyes

ruler

scissors

ballpoint pen

white glue

GLUE

Here is what you do:

1. Draw or trace a 3-inch (8-cm) heart on the cereal box cardboard. Cut the heart out to use as a pattern.

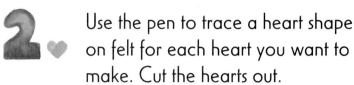

2. Use the pen to trace a heart shape on felt for each heart you want to make. Cut the hearts out.

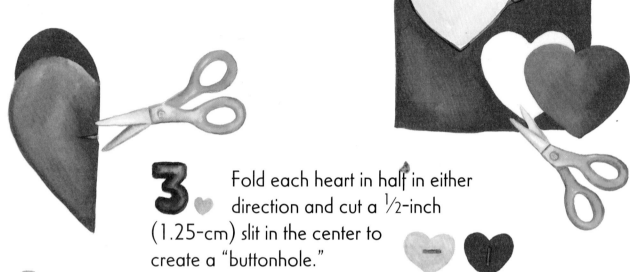

3. Fold each heart in half in either direction and cut a ½-inch (1.25-cm) slit in the center to create a "buttonhole."

4. Use any combination of felt scraps, ribbon, trims, yarn, and wiggle eyes to give each heart a face around the buttonhole, which will become the nose

To wear the heart, slip it over a button on your shirt or blouse.

Don't throw away those old envelopes. They are just
what you need to make these valentine favors.

Envelope Corner Heart Basket

Here is what you need:

envelope

white glue

craft beads

sequins

clamp clothespins

pipe cleaners

tissue paper

scissors

markers

red, pink, or purple construction paper scraps

Here is what you do:

1. Fold one of the bottom corners of the envelope in half. Cut a half heart shape from the fold with the corner of the envelope for the point of the heart. Open the heart up and you will have a paper-heart basket.

2. If you do not like the color of the envelope you used, color both sides of the heart with markers.

3. Cut a handle for the basket from the pipe cleaner. The length will depend upon the size of the heart you cut. Thread some craft beads on the handle to decorate it. Glue the pipe cleaner handle to each side of the basket. If you need to, secure each end of the handle in place with clamp clothespins until the glue has dried.

4. Decorate the outside of the heart basket using cut paper, sequins, or other collage materials.

5. Tuck a square of tissue paper inside the heart basket and fill it with candy hearts.

Envelope heart baskets make great party favors, but they make nice valentine cards, too. Just write your valentine message on the heart basket before you fill it. You might want to put the basket in a baggie and tie it with a pretty ribbon to ensure a safe delivery.

This valentine garland looks very pretty wrapped around a houseplant.

Heart Butterflies Garland

thin red, pink, and purple ribbon

purple, pink, and red construction paper

plastic wrap

scissors

GLUE

white glue

sequins

1 💗 Cut a long piece of thin ribbon for the garland. Make a loop at each end for hanging by folding the end over and knotting it.

Here is what you do:

2 💜 Tear off a strip of plastic wrap as long as the garland. Use this strip as your work surface. The glue will not stick to the plastic wrap when it is dry, making it easier to pick up the garland without tearing the butterflies.

💜 8

3. For each butterfly, cut two 1-inch (2.5-cm) hearts from construction paper.

4. Glue the two points of the hearts together on the ribbon, to form the two wings of the butterfly. Cut two 1-inch (2.5-cm) pieces of thin ribbon and glue them to the center of the butterfly in a V shape so that the two ends stick up to look like antennae. Decorate the wings with sequins.

5. Glue heart butterflies along the entire ribbon. When the glue has dried, tip the wings of each butterfly up slightly.

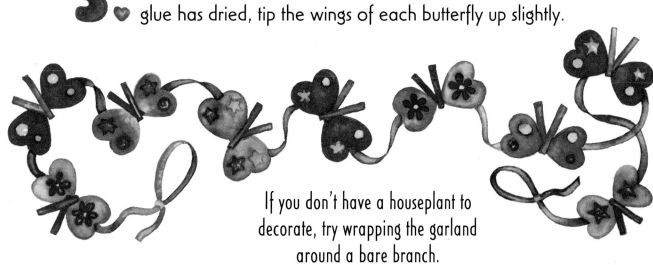

If you don't have a houseplant to decorate, try wrapping the garland around a bare branch.

Brighten your front door with this beautiful bright red wreath.

Plastic Plate Valentine Wreath

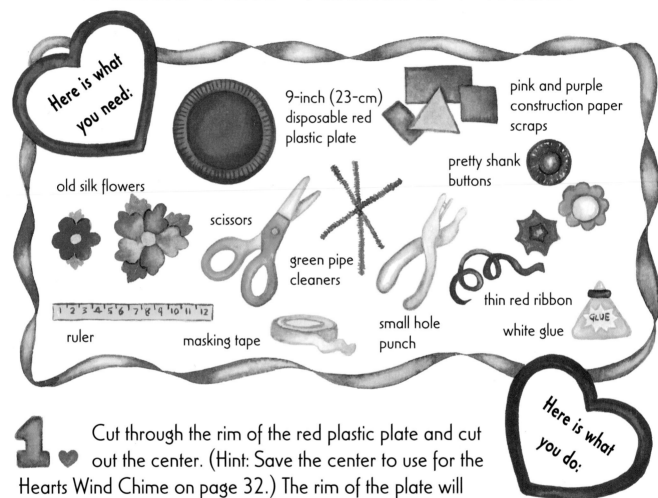

Here is what you need:

9-inch (23-cm) disposable red plastic plate

pink and purple construction paper scraps

pretty shank buttons

old silk flowers

scissors

green pipe cleaners

thin red ribbon

white glue

GLUE

ruler

masking tape

small hole punch

Here is what you do:

1. Cut through the rim of the red plastic plate and cut out the center. (Hint: Save the center to use for the Hearts Wind Chime on page 32.) The rim of the plate will become the wreath.

2. Wrap masking tape around the cut in the rim of the plate to join the rim back together.

3.

Pull the center from one of the silk flowers and take the petals apart.

4. Attach a shank button to one end of a 4-inch (10-cm) piece of green pipe cleaner. Slide a layer of the petals from the silk flower up the pipe cleaner so that it is under the button and the button forms the center of the flower. You can make all sorts of pretty flowers this way. Make three flowers for the wreath.

5.

Twist the ends of the three flowers together and trim off any excess pipe cleaner so that the flowers will lie flat. You might want to glue some leaves cut from the silk flowers behind the three flowers you have made.

6. Cut a 6-inch (15-cm) piece of pipe cleaner. Thread the piece through the stems at the back of the flowers. Then attach the flowers to the wreath over the masking tape by wrapping the ends around the wreath.

7. Punch two small holes, about 5 inches (13 cm) apart, at the top of the wreath. It is important to use two well-spaced holes for the hanger, or the weight of the flowers will tip the wreath to one side. Thread a piece of ribbon through the two holes and tie the ends together to make a hanger.

8.

Cut small hearts from the construction paper scraps and glue them around the wreath to finish decorating it.

The flower decoration on the wreath
also makes a very nice
corsage. Just add a large safety pin
to the back of it.

The tail on this Valentine dog is a lollipop!

Hearts Dog Valentine

Here is what you need:

flat lollipop

thin red ribbon

red, pink, and blue construction paper

stapler

hole punch

scissors

white glue

marker

ruler

Here is what you do:

1. Cut four identical 3-inch (8-cm) hearts from the red construction paper.

2. Cut a slit from the center of the two bumps on one heart to the middle of the heart.

Slide one bump over the other to make a cone and secure with the stapler. This will be the head for the dog, and the point of the cone will be the nose.

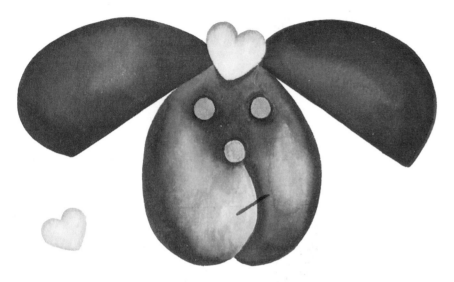

3. Punch a nose for the dog from the pink paper. Glue the nose on the tip of the cone point.

Punch two eyes for the dog from the blue paper. Glue the eyes to the head above the nose.

4. Cut a second heart in half to make the ears for the dog. Staple the tips of the two ears to the top of the head. Cut a small heart from the pink paper to glue over the staple.

5. Staple the edges of the last two hearts together at the bumps and on each side, leaving the pointed ends open, so the hearts make a pocket. This will be the body for the dog.

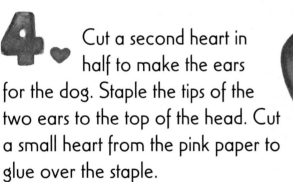

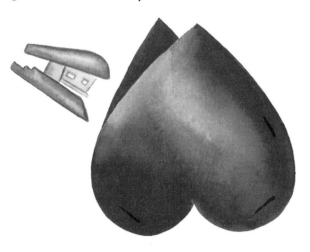

6. Glue the bottom of the head to the point on one side of the hearts pocket.

Cut a small heart from the pink paper and write a short valentine message on it.

7. Tie a piece of the red ribbon in a bow. Glue the bow at the chin of the dog. Glue the small pink heart under the ribbon to look like a dog tag hanging down.

8. Cut a pink heart the size of the lollipop. Write a message on it and sign your name. Glue the heart to the wrapper on one side of the lollipop.

9. Cut a small heart from the pink paper. Write the word "Pull" on the heart. Glue the heart to the end of the lollipop stick. When the glue has dried, tuck the lollipop into the pocket of the dog, making sure that "Pull" shows above his head.

Arf! Arfy!
(Dog talk for "Be mine!")

This valentine can be used all year long.

Valentine Bookmark

Here is what you need:

red card stock or light cardboard

white glue

marker or pen

pink construction paper

scissors

wide lace

heart-shape punch

sticky-back magnet

ruler

Here is what you do:

1. Cut a strip of cardboard about 11 inches (28 cm) long and 2 ½ inches (6 cm) wide.

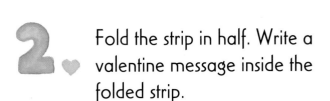

2. Fold the strip in half. Write a valentine message inside the folded strip.

3. Cut two pieces of sticky-back magnet. Stick one piece on the inside of each end of the strip so that the strip will stick together when folded.

4. Close the cardboard strip. Cut a piece of lace to fit over the front and the back of the folded cardboard. Glue the lace over the cardboard.

5. Punch some small hearts from the construction paper and glue them on the lace-covered bookmark to decorate it.

This magnetic valentine bookmark will stick firmly over the page of a book to keep your place.

You have to blow on this valentine to read the hidden message.

Party Blower Valentine

Here is what you need:

party blower (red if possible)

pink construction paper

tiny valentine stickers

heart-shape punch

masking tape

scissors

markers

white glue

GLUE

sequins

Here is what you do:

1. Blow the party blower open and secure the end to your work surface with the masking tape.

2. Decorate the strip with the stickers, tiny cut or punched paper hearts, and sequins.

3. Cut a small heart from the construction paper. Write a valentine message on the heart.

4. Glue the heart to the end of the open party blower so that you will see it when the blower is unrolled.

5. Cut another heart from the construction paper. Use the markers to write: To see my valentine message, blow and draw an arrow pointing down. Glue the heart to the plastic part of the party blower with the arrow pointing to the mouthpiece.

6. When the glue has dried, carefully remove the masking tape and allow the party blower to roll back up.

What a funny way to deliver a valentine message!

Decorate a doorknob with a lacy valentine.

Doorknob Nose Heart

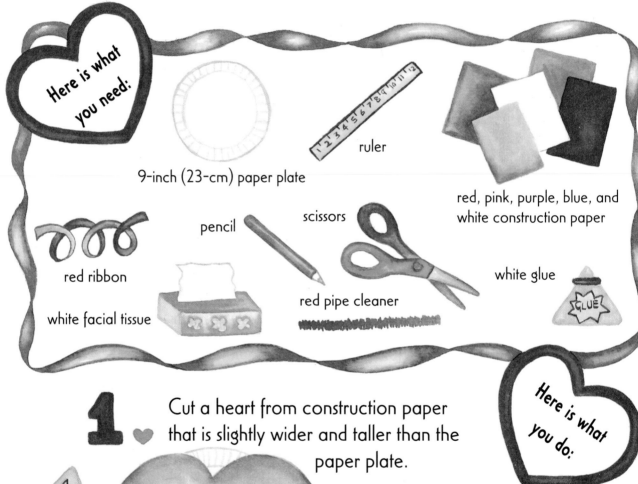

9-inch (23-cm) paper plate

ruler

red, pink, purple, blue, and white construction paper

red ribbon

pencil

scissors

white glue

white facial tissue

red pipe cleaner

1 ♥ Cut a heart from construction paper that is slightly wider and taller than the paper plate.

2 ♥ Glue the heart to the back of the paper plate. Trim away any white part of the plate that is showing around the heart.

3. Cut a 3-inch (8-cm) slit across the center of the heart. Cut another 3-inch (8-cm) slit across the first slit. This will be the place where you will slide the heart over the doorknob.

4. Cut eyes from the construction paper and glue them to the top part of the heart.

5. Cut two heart-shaped cheeks from paper. Glue a cheek on each side of the bottom part of the heart. Bend a 5-inch (13-cm) piece of the red pipe cleaner into a smile. Glue the smile to the bottom part of the heart between the cheeks and overlapping them on each side.

6. Shred some white tissue to make a lacy border on the heart. Squeeze glue around the edge of the heart and press the tissue bits into the glue.

7. Tie a piece of ribbon into a bow. Glue the bow to the top of one side of the heart. Glue a small paper heart to the center of the bow.

Finish the heart by slipping it over a doorknob to give it a big nose.

21

Turn a bunch of hearts upside down to
make a valentine crown in no time.

Hearts Crown

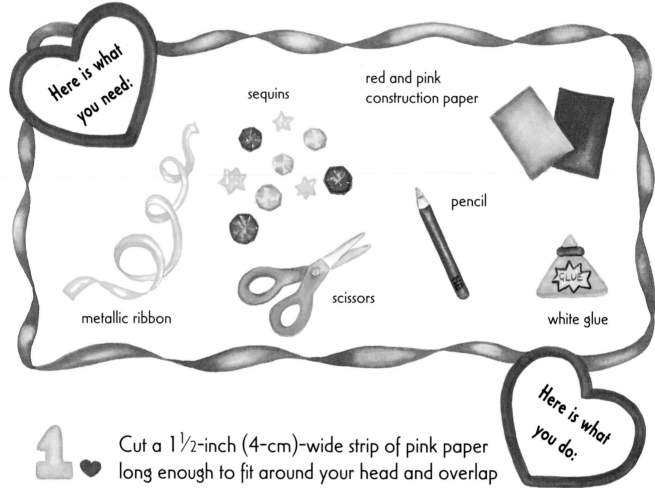

Here is what you need:

sequins

red and pink
construction paper

pencil

metallic ribbon

scissors

white glue

GLUE

Here is what you do:

1. Cut a 1½-inch (4-cm)-wide strip of pink paper
long enough to fit around your head and overlap
to make a band. You may have to glue two strips together.

2. Use the pencil to mark off the space on one end
of the strip that will be covered by the other end
when the band is glued together.

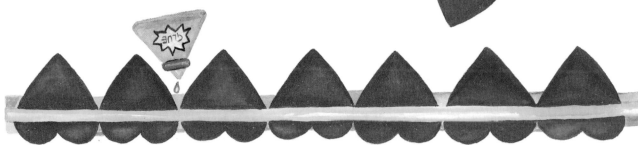

3. ♥ Cut out eight to ten identical 2½-inch (6-cm) hearts from the red paper.

4. ♥ Glue the hearts to the band with the tips up to form the points of the crown.

Glue a strip of metallic ribbon across the bottom part of the crown.

5. ♥ Decorate the tip of each heart with a sequin.

6. ♥

Glue the two ends of the band together to finish the crown.

Crown yourself the king or queen of hearts!

Turn your handprint into a garden of love.

Garden of Love Valentine Holder

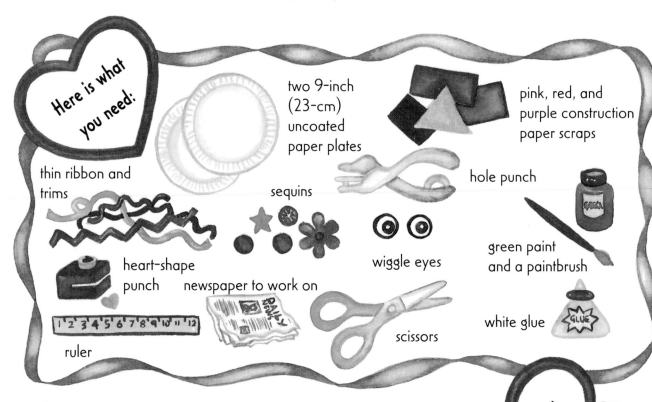

Here is what you need:

two 9-inch (23-cm) uncoated paper plates

pink, red, and purple construction paper scraps

thin ribbon and trims

sequins

hole punch

heart-shape punch

newspaper to work on

wiggle eyes

green paint and a paintbrush

white glue

scissors

ruler

Here is what you do:

1. Paint the palm of your hand green. Make a handprint in the center of the eating side of one of the paper plates.

2. Each of your fingers will be a stem for the heart flowers. You can cut hearts from paper or punch several tiny hearts to use as the petals for a flower with a sequin center. You might want to give one of the flowers a happy face with wiggle eyes and a sequin nose. Use the ideas shown or your own ideas to make each flower different.

3. Cut straight across the second paper plate about 4 inches (10 cm) in from the edge.

4. Turn the smaller piece cut from the plate over and glue it edge to edge with the first plate across the bottom of the handprint to make a pocket.

5. Decorate the edges of the plate carrier by gluing on pretty trims.

6. Punch a hole in the top of the carrier. Thread an 8-inch (20-cm) length of the thin ribbon through the hole. Tie the ends together to make a hanger for the carrier.

This project also makes a very nice coupon holder to give to your mom for a Valentine's Day present.

Leave your true love a different message each day!

Changing Message Magnet

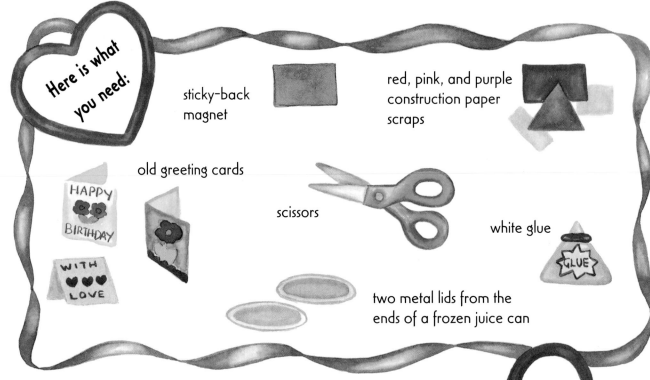

Here is what you need:

sticky-back magnet

red, pink, and purple construction paper scraps

old greeting cards

scissors

white glue

two metal lids from the ends of a frozen juice can

Here is what you do:

1. Cut a heart from paper slightly bigger than the metal lid. It does not need to cover the lid.

2. Glue the heart to the indented side of one of the lids.

LOVE ♥ LOVE ♥ LOVE

3. ♥ Find words you might like to use for your messages in the old greeting cards. Cut the words out. Stick them to pieces of sticky-back magnet, then trim around them.

 HUGS

HAPPY XX KISSES♥

VALENTINE LOVE MY

TO hello

4. ♥ Cut some tiny hearts to use with the words. Stick each heart to a piece of sticky-back magnet, then trim around the heart.

Hug

5. ♥

Put a piece of sticky-back magnet on the backs of both lids.

Stick all the words and hearts on the plain lid to keep them together. Stick both lids on the refrigerator. Select words from the plain lid to write messages on the heart. Add some tiny hearts for decoration. Change the message often.

Make a wearable valentine from a rubber band.

Rubber Band Valentine Bracelets

Here is what you need:

3½-inch (9-cm) flat-sided rubber bands

heart-shape punch

paper scraps

ultrafine-point permanent markers

white glue

GLUE

craft gems and sequins

Here is what you do:

1. Use the permanent markers to write a valentine message inside the rubber band.

happy valentines day love Barbara

happy valentines day love Barbara xx

2. Decorate the outside of the rubber band with the markers.

x love and kisses x x

3. Decorate the outside of the rubber band by gluing on craft gems, sequins, or punched paper hearts.

For you on valentines day

Hugs and kisses
xx x David x xx

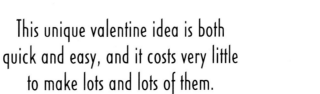

Lots of love on valentines day xxx

This unique valentine idea is both quick and easy, and it costs very little to make lots and lots of them.

Give all your friends both candy and flowers this Valentine's Day.

Candy Flower Valentine

Here is what you need:

red, pink, or purple construction paper

hole punch

clear plastic wrap

green construction paper

round lollipop

scissors

ruler

white glue

marker or pen

Here is what you do:

1 ❤ Cut six 3-inch (8-cm) hearts from any combination of the red, pink, or purple paper.

2 ❤ Punch a hole in the point of each heart.

3. Unwrap the lollipop. Rewrap it in a 4-inch (10-cm) square of clear plastic wrap so that the color shows through. Twist the wrap around the stick to get it as close to the stick as possible.

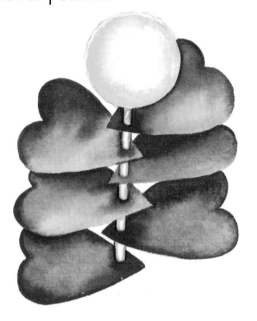

4. Slide the hearts onto the lollipop stick and work them up over the plastic wrap so that they are under the lollipop candy. Arrange the hearts around the lollipop like the petals of a flower.

5. Cut two 3-inch (8-cm) hearts from the green paper to use for the leaves of the flower.

6. Use the pen or marker to write a valentine message on one leaf and sign your name on the other one.

7. Glue the leaves on each side of the lollipop stick.

Try writing a valentine pun for your flower like, "Valentine, I'd 'flower' you anywhere." Get it? I said "flower" instead of "follow." Hee hee!

Here is a decoration you can hang inside or out.

Hearts Wind Chime

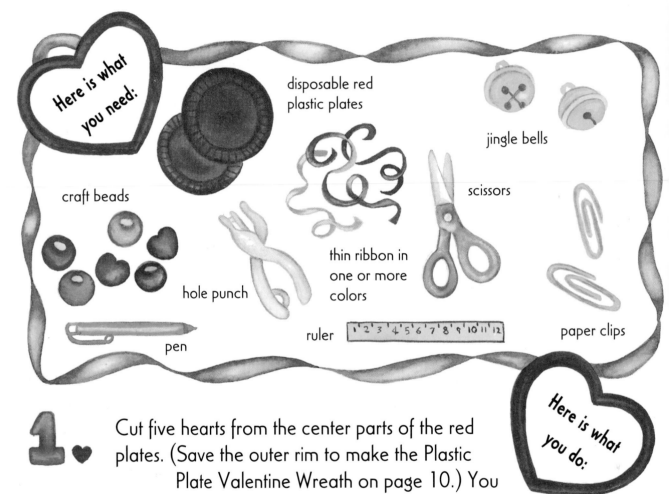

Here is what you need:

disposable red plastic plates

jingle bells

craft beads

scissors

hole punch

thin ribbon in one or more colors

paper clips

pen

ruler

Here is what you do:

1. ♥ Cut five hearts from the center parts of the red plates. (Save the outer rim to make the Plastic Plate Valentine Wreath on page 10.) You can cut them freehand or use the pen to trace a heart pattern on the plastic. The hearts can be the same or different sizes.

2. ♥ Use the hole punch to make a hole at the top and the bottom of each heart.

♥ 32

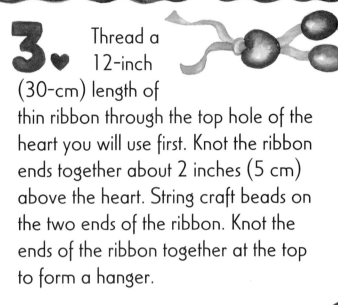

3. Thread a 12-inch (30-cm) length of thin ribbon through the top hole of the heart you will use first. Knot the ribbon ends together about 2 inches (5 cm) above the heart. String craft beads on the two ends of the ribbon. Knot the ends of the ribbon together at the top to form a hanger.

4. Slide a paper clip through the hole at the bottom of the first heart. Attach a second heart to the first by hanging it on the other end of the same paper clip. Continue to add hearts and paper clips until all the hearts are attached in a row.

5. Cut three 12-inch (30-cm) lengths of thin ribbon. Thread the ends of the three ribbons through the bottom hole in the last heart until both ends of the ribbons are of equal length. Thread two craft beads over all six ribbon ends and slide the beads up to the heart. Knot the ribbons under the beads.

6. Tie a craft bead or jingle bell to the ends of the ribbons.

Find a breezy place to hang the hearts and listen to the sound of the soft jingle.

Are you ready for the heart races?

Racing Hearts Game

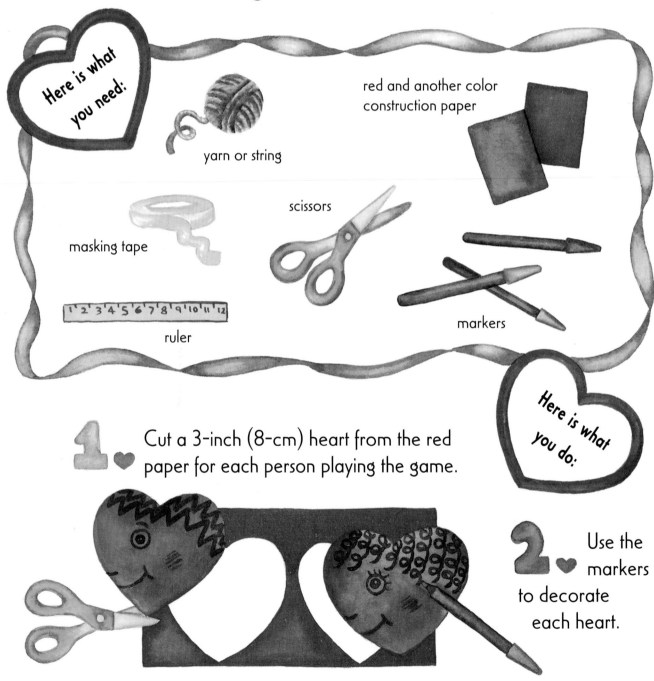

Here is what you need:

yarn or string

red and another color construction paper

masking tape

scissors

ruler

markers

Here is what you do:

1. Cut a 3-inch (8-cm) heart from the red paper for each person playing the game.

2. Use the markers to decorate each heart.

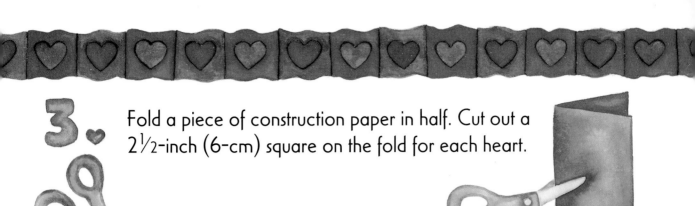

3. Fold a piece of construction paper in half. Cut out a 2½-inch (6-cm) square on the fold for each heart.

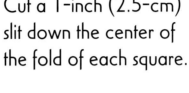

4. Cut a 1-inch (2.5-cm) slit down the center of the fold of each square.

DAVID   JULIA

5. Write the name of the person racing the heart on each square.

6. Slip the point of a heart into the slit of a square. Spread the fold of the square open on the bottom so that it stands up.

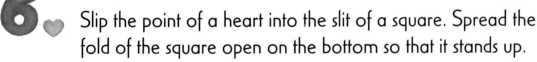

7. Find a smooth surface to race on. Cut a long piece of string or yarn to mark the starting line and another to mark the finish line of the race. Secure the ends of the lines with the masking tape.

DAVID

JULIA

To play the game, each person blows on his or her own heart to try to move it to the finish line first. You can also create wind to move the hearts by using paper fans or by squeezing empty plastic detergent bottles.

This project is both a valentine and a small gift.

Message Pad Valentine

Here is what you need:

poster board

small pad of sticky notes

ribbon and trims

marker

red construction paper

heart-shape punch

scissors

white glue

sticky-back magnet

pretty wrapping paper

ruler

Here is what you do:

1. Cut a 6½ by 3¼ -inch (16.5 by 8.25-cm) strip of poster board.

2. Fold the strip in half to make a cover for the notepad.

3. Cover the poster board with pretty wrapping paper. Be sure to do this with the poster board strip folded over, or the paper will pull on the ends when you try to fold it.

4. Glue the notepad to the back of the inside of the cover.

5. Use ribbon, trims, and punched hearts to decorate the front of the cover to look like a valentine gift.

6. Put a piece of sticky-back magnet on the back of the cover so the pad can be hung on the refrigerator.

7. Use the marker to write your valentine message on the first page of the pad inside the cover.

This makes a great gift for teachers.

This jewelry craft makes a tasty party favor.

Valentine Candy Jewelry

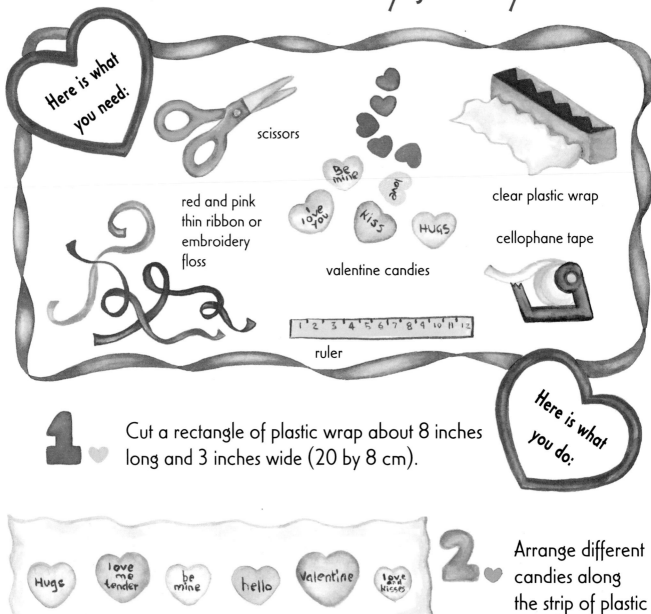

Here is what you need:

scissors

red and pink thin ribbon or embroidery floss

valentine candies

ruler

clear plastic wrap

cellophane tape

Here is what you do:

1. Cut a rectangle of plastic wrap about 8 inches long and 3 inches wide (20 by 8 cm).

2. Arrange different candies along the strip of plastic wrap.

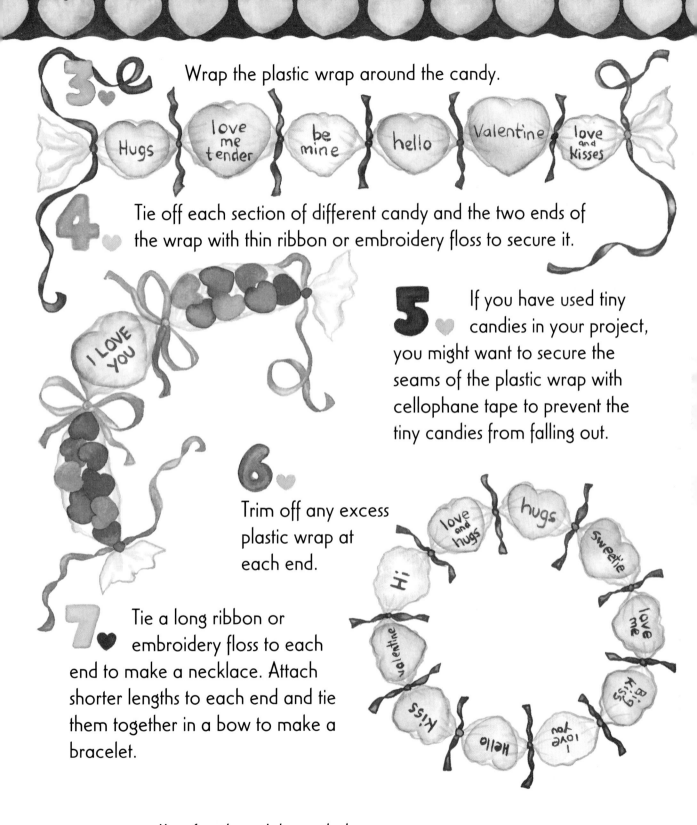

3.e Wrap the plastic wrap around the candy.

Hugs · love me tender · be mine · hello · Valentine · love and kisses

4. Tie off each section of different candy and the two ends of the wrap with thin ribbon or embroidery floss to secure it.

I LOVE YOU

5. If you have used tiny candies in your project, you might want to secure the seams of the plastic wrap with cellophane tape to prevent the tiny candies from falling out.

6. Trim off any excess plastic wrap at each end.

7. Tie a long ribbon or embroidery floss to each end to make a necklace. Attach shorter lengths to each end and tie them together in a bow to make a bracelet.

love and hugs · hugs · sweetie · love me · Big Kiss · I love you · Hello · kiss · valentine · Hi

Your friends won't know whether to wear these valentine favors or eat them.

Turn penny wrappers into tiny heart-shaped baskets for
"sweetheart" cinnamon candies.

Penny Wrapper Heart Basket

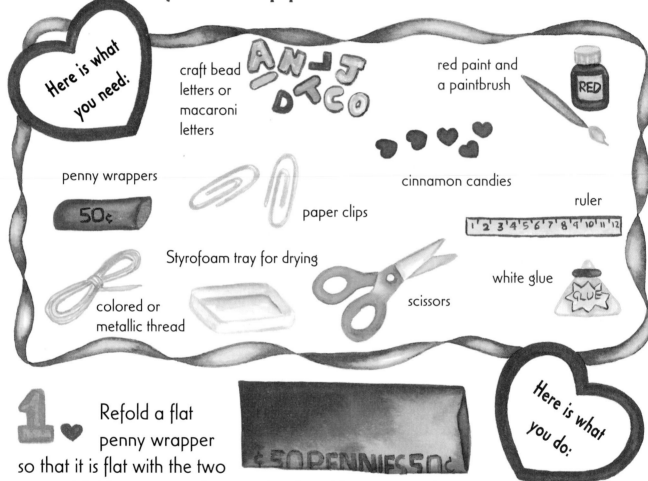

Here is what you need:

craft bead letters or macaroni letters

red paint and a paintbrush

penny wrappers

50¢

paper clips

cinnamon candies

ruler

Styrofoam tray for drying

white glue

colored or metallic thread

scissors

1. Refold a flat penny wrapper so that it is flat with the two original fold seams touching each other. The print on the wrapper will now be folded down the center.

Here is what you do:

2. Fold the wrapper in half from top to bottom. Round off the open ends of the penny wrapper to look like one bump of a heart.

♥ 40

3. Unfold the wrapper and flatten it out to the original fold, with the writing on the front.

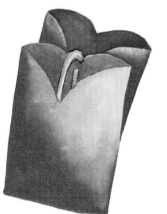

4. Fold the wrapper in half across the center to make the heart basket. Secure the fold with a dab of glue. Slide a paper clip over the center to hold the folded heart together.

5. You can paint the heart bright red or leave it the red color of the penny wrapper. If you paint the basket, let it dry on the Styrofoam tray.

6. You can glue a message to the front of the heart basket using craft bead letters or macaroni letters.

7. String a 6-inch (13-cm) piece of thread through the top of the paper clip. Tie the ends of the thread together to make a hanger for the basket.

8. Fill the basket with "sweetheart" cinnamon candies. If you are giving the basket as a gift, put a square of plastic wrap around the candies tied with a pretty ribbon. This will keep the candy fresh and prevent it from spilling out of the basket.

If you are making several baskets for party favors, you might want to display the baskets by hanging them from a bare branch.

Get your valentines by priority mail.

Priority Mail Box Valentines Holder

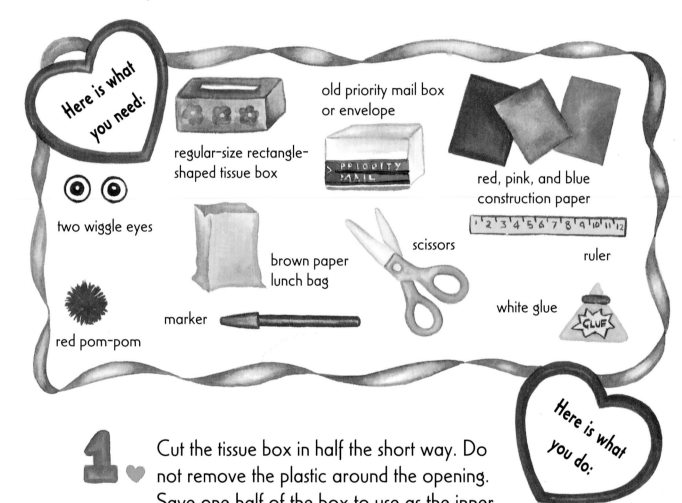

Here is what you need:

regular-size rectangle-shaped tissue box

old priority mail box or envelope

red, pink, and blue construction paper

two wiggle eyes

brown paper lunch bag

scissors

ruler

red pom-pom

marker

white glue

GLUE

1. Cut the tissue box in half the short way. Do not remove the plastic around the opening. Save one half of the box to use as the inner container for the mail box.

Here is what you do:

42

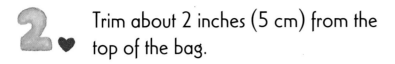

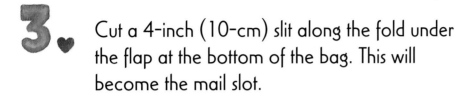

2. Trim about 2 inches (5 cm) from the top of the bag.

3. Cut a 4-inch (10-cm) slit along the fold under the flap at the bottom of the bag. This will become the mail slot.

4. Turn the box half so that the opening is at the top. Open the bag and slip it over the box.

5. Cut a 4- by 5-inch (10- by 13-cm) rectangle from the blue paper. Round off two corners on the long side to form the top of the mail box.

6. Glue the blue mail box top to the bottom of the bag, which now forms the top of the mail box. Be careful not to glue the flap shut over the mail slot.

7. Glue the two wiggle eyes and the pom-pom for a nose to the blue paper.

8. Cut one of the red, white, and blue strips from the priority mail box that says "Priority Mail." Make the strip long enough to go all the way across the bottom part of the mail box. Glue the strip in place.

9. Cut a heart from the red paper. Use the marker to write the words: "Lift flap to mail" on the heart. Glue the heart to the front of the mail box.

10. Decorate the mail box with additional hearts cut from paper. Write your name on one of the hearts so everyone will know whose mail box it is.

To use the mail box holder, lift up the flap of the mail box and drop the mail into the box. To empty the mail box, slide the bag off the box and dump the valentines out. Mail call!

Make someone special some valentine flowers.

Hearts and Buttons Flowers

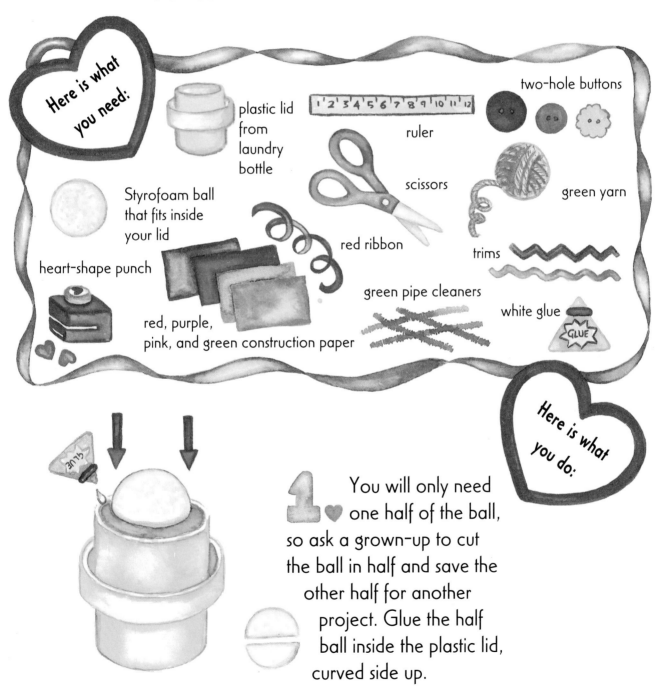

plastic lid from laundry bottle

ruler

two-hole buttons

Styrofoam ball that fits inside your lid

scissors

green yarn

heart-shape punch

red ribbon

trims

green pipe cleaners

white glue

red, purple, pink, and green construction paper

GLUE

Here is what you do:

1 You will only need one half of the ball, so ask a grown-up to cut the ball in half and save the other half for another project. Glue the half ball inside the plastic lid, curved side up.

45

2. To make each flower, cut a 4- to 6-inch (10- to 15-cm) stem from the green pipe cleaners.

3. Thread one end of the stem through the hole in one of the buttons, then bend it down and push it through the second hole. Bend the end to secure the button to the stem. The button will be the center of the flower.

4. Punch five or more hearts from construction paper to use as petals for the flower. If you don't have a heart-shape punch, you can use a scissors to cut out little hearts from the construction paper.

5. Glue the points of each heart around the underside of the button. Make at least five button flowers. Let the glue dry before continuing.

6. ♥ Cut snips of green yarn and glue them to the Styrofoam ball to make it seem covered with grass.

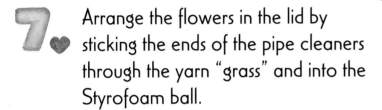

7. ♥ Arrange the flowers in the lid by sticking the ends of the pipe cleaners through the yarn "grass" and into the Styrofoam ball.

8. ♥ Punch some heart-shaped leaves for the flowers from the green paper. Glue the leaves to the pipe-cleaner stems.

9. ♥ Glue pretty trim around the plastic lid to decorate it. Tie the red ribbon in a bow around the top of the lid.

How pretty!

About the Author and Illustrator

Thirty years as a teacher and director of nursery school programs have given Kathy Ross extensive experience in guiding young children through craft projects. Among the more than forty craft books she has written are Crafts for All Seasons, Crafts from Your Favorite Children's Songs, Kathy Ross Crafts Letter Shapes, The Best Christmas Crafts Ever!, and Play-Doh™ Fun and Games. To find out more about Kathy, visit her Web site: www.kathyross.com.

Barbara Leonard is a freelance designer who is now working in Italy. She has designed all sorts of products, including wallpaper, fabrics, rugs, beach towels, gift wrap, greeting cards, and children's bedding. One of her mug designs is on permanent exhibit in the Victoria and Albert Museum in London. This is the first time Barbara has turned her design talents to the pages of a children's book.